TENSES

TENSES

THE SERIAL INTELLECTUAL

Serial Intellectual, LLC

CONTENTS

CHAPTER 1

INTRODUCTION

I am very excited about this book because it will help many people come to grips with and navigate through what we are all experiencing as we try to live our lives.

The past, the future, and the present are all realities we deal with consciously or subconsciously. They are either friends creating drama in an all-out war or experiencing peace; when they are at their best, they can develop a utopia for us.

Tenses tell the story of three individuals: PAST, FUTURE, and PRESENT. It chronicles their upbringing, their early adult lives, and everything else. Bringing them to life has been a joy, a pleasure, and a beautiful, artistic way to learn.

This book on tenses is so important to me because I have battled with the past, the future, and the present for most of my adult life. The thing is, for so many years, I didn't even know what was going on, and as I began to understand that these three tenses were at work within me, I began to have a little hope, but still, I had no tools or training to deal with them. It wasn't until the pain caused by the war between them got so deep that it forced me to begin to do some work and create some tools to help me deal with them.

I have spent the last twelve years applying these tools and the concepts and principles you will find in this book on myself and others with profound results. I am beyond excited to introduce this book to the world, hoping that many individuals will experience the transformation they long for and that the world will be a better place.

I want to thank God for the wisdom he has given me and my family and friends. He surrounded me with them, and all the opportunities I've had up to this point in my life are all beautiful gifts from Him and Him alone. I say thank you.

But I want to say special thanks to Keith and Adriane Davis, who have walked with me through one of the most difficult times in my life, and in so many ways, they have been the past, the future, and the present for me. I am convinced that this book would've never made it to print without their influence in my life; they are the type of friends every person needs.

Finally, I want to say thank you to Lareine. My serial intellectual assistant magic happens when two or more people come together with shared values, good character, and honed skills, and the writing of *Tenses* perfectly illustrates all of this. For a large portion of my life, I have prayed for and looked for a person to team up with to bring my intellectual products to life so that they can help transform people and change the world. I want to say thank you, my friend, for making my dreams come true; you are a light in a dark world and one of the most encouraging people I've ever met.

CHAPTER 2

FRIENDS

In a charming park surrounded by vibrant blossoms and towering trees, three children with peculiar names—PAST, FUTURE, and PRESENT—encountered one another for the first time. PAST, a nostalgic and reflective soul, was always lost in old stories and cherished memories. FUTURE, with eyes sparkling with dreams, constantly pondered the possibilities that lie ahead. PRESENT, a lively and spontaneous spirit, embraced every moment with infectious enthusiasm.

It was a fateful afternoon when they crossed paths, drawn to a solitary oak tree that seemed to whisper secrets from centuries past. Each child had sought refuge under its branches, and as they exchanged curious glances, an unspoken bond formed between them. From that day on, they became inseparable.

Under the oak tree's sheltering branches, PAST, FUTURE, and PRESENT found themselves engrossed in a peculiar activity. They had brought with them a collection of old trinkets and keepsakes, which they carefully laid out on a worn-out quilt spread beneath the tree.

PRESENT, with vibrant eyes and infectious energy, was the first to speak up. "Look what I found today!" PRESENT held up a beautifully crafted antique pocket watch. Its golden casing reflected the sunlight.

PAST's eyes lit up with recognition. "That's a vintage timepiece! Oh, how it reminds me of my grandparents. They used to have one just like it." PAST traced the watch's engravings gently, lost in a swirl of memories.

FUTURE leaned in, intrigued by the watch. "Do you think it still works?" they wondered aloud.

PRESENT grinned mischievously. "Let's find out!" PRESENT carefully wound the watch, and to their delight, the hands began to move and its delicate ticking sound filled their ears, measuring the passage of time once more. "Look at that! It's like we've brought a piece of the past back to life."

They continued to explore the treasures they had brought—a weathered diary filled with handwritten notes, a vintage camera that still held a roll of film, and a stack of old postcards from exotic locations around the world.

As they delved into the objects, they began to uncover the stories behind each one. PAST shared tales of bygone eras, weaving vivid pictures of historical events while FUTURE envisioned the adventures that lay ahead, imagining the possibilities that the world held for them.

PAST looked at FUTURE, captivated by the fire in their eyes, found inspired by the sense of endless possibilities that radiated from the new friend. FUTURE, in turn, felt a sense of grounding in the presence of PAST, realizing that they needed a strong foundation to become reality.

PRESENT, sensing the unspoken emotions, nudged them closer together. "Isn't it fascinating?" they exclaimed. "We all see the world in different ways, but we are here, together, in this very moment, beneath this beautiful tree."

The others nodded in agreement, their unspoken bond deepening, discovering that each had something unique to offer. PAST found comfort in sharing tales; FUTURE, in return, ignited PAST's imagination with visions of journeys they had never thought possible. PRESENT, as the glue that held them together, reveled in the joy of their newfound friendship.

Under the oak tree's watchful eye, time seemed to stand still as the hours slipped away unnoticed. As the sun began its descent, casting a golden glow over the park, they realized how effortlessly they complemented each other. It was as if the universe had orchestrated their meeting to remind them that past, present, and future were not isolated fragments, but threads intricately woven into the tapestry of existence.

With the setting sun as their witness, they made a silent vow—a promise to support one another, to learn from the past, to dream of the future, and to cherish every moment in the present. From that day on, their lives became entwined in a beautiful dance, and they knew they were no longer alone in navigating the grand adventure of life.

As they ventured into adolescence, their friendship only deepened. Together, they faced the challenges of growing up—heartbreaks, uncertainties, and the ever-pressing question of what the future held for them. Yet, their bond remained unshakable, like the roots intertwining beneath the oak tree that had witnessed their journey.

One summer evening, the trio sat beneath their faithful oak tree. PAST, with a tinge of sadness in the eyes, spoke softly, "I fear that our past will become too heavy for me to carry. What if I am defined by my fears and cannot break free from them?"

FUTURE, with eyes full of encouragement, replied, "Do not be afraid, dear friend. The past shapes us, but it does not define us. We are the authors of our own destinies, and together, we can create a future that defies any biased notions."

PRESENT chimed in, "Absolutely! And don't forget, the present is a gift. Embrace each moment, for it is an opportunity to make choices that will lead us toward the future we desire."

Their reassuring words comforted PAST, and they smiled gratefully. It was in these moments of vulnerability that their bond grew even stronger.

One spring, as the park bloomed with the promise of new beginnings, PAST, FUTURE, and PRESENT decided to embark on a heartwarming project together. They would plant a beautiful flower garden, a living symbol of their blossoming friendship and the growth of their dreams.

They began their endeavor with shovels in hand and hearts full of anticipation. PAST carefully chose heritage seeds that held the stories of their ancestors and represented the beauty of the past. FUTURE selected exotic and rare blooms, reflecting their own daring spirit and the adventures ahead. PRESENT, in a high-spirited way, added an array of vibrant and cheerful flowers, capturing the essence of their shared joyful moments.

They worked side by side, united in their vision, planting each seed and nurturing the delicate sprouts with love and care. As they tended to the garden, their bond grew stronger, and their laughter filled the air like the sweet scent of flowers.

Word spread like wildfire through the town about the captivating garden created by the three extraordinary friends. The vibrant colors and enchanting aroma drew visitors from far and wide, but it was not just the beauty of the flowers that captivated them; it was also the undeniable sense of unity and harmony that radiated from PAST, FUTURE, and PRESENT.

Inspired by their friendship, others began to see the value in embracing all aspects of time—the wisdom of the past, the potential of the future, and the joy of the present. The garden became a place of solace, where people sought refuge from their daily worries.

As the years passed, the garden flourished, much like the friendship of PAST, FUTURE, and PRESENT. It became a gathering place for storytelling, a haven where people of different ages and backgrounds came together, connected by a shared appreciation for the passage of time and the beauty of the present moment.

Each season, the garden transformed, mirroring the changing landscapes of their lives. The blooms of spring symbolized new beginnings, the lush greens of summer embodied growth and vitality, the warm hues of autumn celebrated the richness of experiences, and the serenity of winter reflected the wisdom that came with reflection.

But the true magic of the garden was not just in its appearance; it lay in the friendships it fostered. Many a heart found solace under the oak tree and amid the flowers, and countless dreams were nurtured, taking root in the fertile soil of their minds.

PAST, FUTURE, and PRESENT knew that their friendship was a gift to cherish, and they made sure to carve out time for one another to water the garden of their bond with love and understanding.

CHAPTER 2: DRAMA

As they grew old, their close friendship faced its first real test. The perspectives that had brought them together now seemed to clash. PAST began to view FUTURE's perspective as impractical and far-fetched. FUTURE, on the other hand, saw PRESENT as overly fixated, accusing PAST of dwelling on what was gone instead of enjoying the present moment.

This trio found itself caught in a cycle of anger and resentment. PAST grew increasingly frustrated with FUTURE and PRESENT for not understanding their concerns. It felt like their opinions were being brushed aside, causing them to withdraw from the friendship. PAST found themself tangled in a web of mounting frustration intertwined with these entities known as FUTURE and PRESENT. Their stubbornness and seeming reluctance to grasp the depth of PAST's concerns only heightened their turmoil. Heavy-hearted, the wounds of trauma carried a burden of emotions like a whisper lost in eternity's expanse. The vibrant voice now yearned to be heard and understood, but it felt like the pain was merely discarded like forgotten relics from an era. The scars of abuse were etched into the very fabric of their being, a silent testimony to the struggles they had endured. The weight of memories held PAST captive, a constant reminder of the past wishing to escape.

On the other hand, FUTURE grew increasingly offended with PAST's resistance to dreams. To FUTURE's dismay, it appeared that PRESENT struggled to embrace the brilliance of aspirations. FUTURE yearned for their support and recognition, hoping that they would peer into the realm of possibility with the same fervors FUTURE did. However, instead of finding encouragement, FUTURE perceived a veil of skepticism and hesitation, an invisible wall that stifled the momentum. This caused FUTURE to distance from the group, seeking solace in pursuing their dreams elsewhere.

PRESENT, stuck in the middle of the conflict, felt torn between the two friends. PRESENT tried to mediate, but each time they attempted to bring peace, PRESENT was caught in the crossfire of their arguments. The pressure to keep the group together weighed heavily, and they began to withdraw, feeling overwhelmed and unsupported. PRESENT could perceive the allure of FUTURE's desire, with the intoxicating promise of tomorrow's greatness, and PRESENT could comprehend the depth of PAST's convictions, grounded in the wisdom of yesterday. Yet, in their own earnest endeavor to bridge the gap between these two formidable entities, PRESENT was entangled in escalating disputes. Each attempt at mediation felt like a minefield, with words serving as fragile bridges across the misunderstanding.

The arguments became more frequent and intense, and the once-strong bond among the three friends seemed to wither away. Each of them became more stubborn and less willing to see things from the others' perspectives.

One day, during a particularly heated argument, PAST shouted, "I can't take this anymore! You both refuse to understand where I'm coming from. I'm done trying to make you see the reason."

FUTURE retorted, "You're just stuck in the past, unable to see the possibilities of the future. We don't need you holding us back."

PRESENT spoke up, frustration evident in their voice. "You both need to stop living in your own worlds and acknowledge what's happening right here, right now. PAST, you keep bringing up the past as if it's the only thing that matters. FUTURE, you're always lost in your dreams, and it's getting annoying."

FUTURE retorted sharply, "Well, maybe if you weren't so focused on the present, you'd realize the potential for something greater in the future. Your obsession with instant gratification blinds you from seeing the bigger picture!"

PAST crossed his arms defensively. "I'm not stuck in the past; I just appreciate the memories we've shared. But I can't stand your constant daydreaming, FUTURE. It's like you're never fully present with us."

The accusations flew back and forth, and it seemed like they were digging themselves deeper into the rift that had formed between them. PAST, FUTURE, and PRESENT were all firm in their beliefs, and none was willing to back down.

Suddenly, PAST stood up, their eyes narrowed with anger. "I've had enough of this. If you both can't understand and respect my perspective, then maybe this friendship isn't worth saving."

FUTURE's expression hardened and they rose to their feet as well. "Fine. Maybe you're right. I don't need friends who can't appreciate my passion."

But they were all too angry to listen, and the argument escalated further. Hurtful words were exchanged, and in the heat of the moment, they decided to take a break from each other. They parted ways, each feeling hurt, misunderstood, and resentful.

One day, PAST found themselves at their favorite spot, a peaceful park where the trio had spent countless hours talking and laughing together. Sitting on a bench, PAST recalled the good times they had shared, and a sense of nostalgia washed over them. PAST realized that while valuing the past, they have also been resistant to change, to the natural evolution of their lives and friendships.

At the same time, FUTURE was pushing forward, making strides toward their goals, but couldn't help feeling a sense of loneliness. Achieving small victories, FUTURE missed having friends to share the excitement with and realized that dreams seemed more fulfilling with their support.

PRESENT, stuck in indecision, longed for the days when they were all united. The weight of trying to mend their broken friendship rested heavily on their shoulders. They knew ignoring the past or dismissing the future wouldn't help. PRESENT understood that holding onto resentment wouldn't bring them back together.

A sudden and sinister transformation began to unfold as PAST, FUTURE, and PRESENT gazed back at the flower garden they had once cultivated with hope and unity. The once-enchanting garden, a symbol of their blooming friendship, now bore the weight of a dark aura that seemed to seep into every petal and leaf.

The mysterious ailment that had befallen the flowers appeared to mirror the distress that had crept into their once-harmonious camaraderie. The fading blooms now reflected the fading connection between the three entities, as if the garden itself mirrored the turmoil within their hearts.

With each passing day, the flowers withered further, and their once-glorious colors dimmed into melancholy shades as though the very essence of their friendship was being drained away. The bittersweet beauty that once adorned the garden now became a haunting reminder of what it once was.

The affliction spread as the garden transformed into a dark and ominous place, causing other flowers nearby to wither and die. The symbolism was stark, signifying that the deterioration of their friendship was not an isolated event but had repercussions that echoed far beyond their realm.

Each trio member could sense the heavy burden of responsibility for the state of the garden and their friendship. The dark aura over the garden manifested the unresolved conflicts and miscommunication that had taken root within their relationship.

CHAPTER 3

WAR

The tension between PAST, FUTURE, and PRESENT reached its boiling point, and the once-harmonious park became a battleground of clashing personalities. The ground trembled beneath their conflicting views, and the air was hostile.

PAST, with a furrowed brow and a deep sense of responsibility, recalled past mistakes and attempted to impose life lessons on their friends. It believed that understanding history was crucial to avoid the same pitfalls in the future. Their voice echoed with the wisdom of ages gone by, and they felt a duty to guide their friends away from repeating the errors of the past.

"Why can't they see the significance of the past? Trauma and abuse are cruel teachers, and I've learned the lessons the hard way. I carry the weight of our mistakes, and it's my responsibility to ensure they don't repeat those errors. They must understand the consequences of their actions and the decisions they make. My friends may not always appreciate my caution, but I can't bear to watch them stumble into the same traps that once ensnared me. If only they'd listen and learn from what's already happened, they might spare themselves the pain and turmoil that I've endured."

FUTURE, equally determined and with unwavering ambition, envisioned strategies to avoid past mistakes by dismissing PAST's cautionary tales. They felt that dwelling on yesterday was holding them back, and they were eager to charge into the future with unbridled optimism. Their eyes gleamed with the excitement of unexplored frontiers.

"Why is PAST so fixated on what's already done? The past is just that—a thing of the past. Dwelling on the trauma and abuse that shaped it is a waste of time. The real potential lies in the future, and I'm determined to reach it. There's so much to explore, so many possibilities to seize. I'm not afraid to take risks and push boundaries. My friends may think I'm reckless, but I'm driven by my vision for what's ahead. I refuse to let the scars of the past hold me back. The future is ours for the taking."

Caught in the middle, PRESENT darted between their friends, trying to keep the peace but imposing their belief that they were both wrong. They argued that they lived in idealized worlds, missing the most important aspect—the present. PRESENT wanted them to embrace the joys of the here and now and not be burdened by the past or constrained by the future.

"Why do they have to be so stubborn? Can't they see the value in balancing the past and the future with the present? I understand that the wisdom of the past is essential, and the excitement of the future is enticing. But they're missing the point—the here and now matters too. There's beauty in the moment, in the present experiences and connections. Life is fleeting, and we need to appreciate every second of it. I want them to embrace the joy of living in the present and cherish what's right in front of them without being burdened by regrets or ambition. If only they could find that balance, it'd be much easier for us all."

Their emotions spiraled out of control, and they hurled words at each other like weapons, their once-strong bond withering under the weight of ego and stubbornness.

"You're stuck in the past, refusing to see the potential of the future!" FUTURE accused, their voice sharp with frustration. "You keep carrying the weight of trauma and abuse as if they define you. But there's so much more to who you are and who you can become. Embrace the lessons without letting them imprison you. Don't let the shadows of yesterday overshadow the brilliance of tomorrow."

PAST's eyes flashed with indignation. "The trauma and abuse I've endured are not just burdens to be cast aside. They are part of my story, shaping the person I've become. Ignoring them would be a disservice to me and to others who have faced similar struggles. Acknowledging the past doesn't mean I'm stuck; it means I'm learning, growing, and using those experiences to build a better future."

PRESENT interjected, "Both of you are blind to the wonders of the present! We need to focus on what's happening right now! Let's not let our fixation on either extreme rob us of the richness of the present experience."

As the battle raged on, their egos seemed to fortify their positions, and the possibility of reconciliation became more distant with each passing moment.

In their pride, they failed to see that their differences were not weaknesses to overcome, but strengths that could complement each other. The beauty of their friendship was buried beneath the rubble of their discord, and it seemed that war was indeed inevitable.

With each passing argument, the bonds that had once woven them together grew weaker. Their garden, once a symbol of unity, withered under the stress of their discord. As PAST sat in quiet contemplation, a shadowy figure materialized nearby, and PAST's gaze locked onto the distant horizon. The presence seemed to carry an air of frustration, as if they bore the weight of unspoken anger. The figure's words held a certain edge, encouraging PAST to channel the pent-up emotions toward the present and the future.

"Look at them." The figure's words dripped with bitterness and resentment. "They wander through life oblivious to the pain we've endured. Their dreams are unfettered by the trauma and abuse that have marked our past." PAST felt a stirring within, a sense of solidarity with the figure's perspective. The wounds resonated with the figure's resentment, forming an unexpected connection.

FUTURE wandered the desolate park, hopeful eyes now clouded with despair. Beneath a canopy of trees, they sank to the ground, burying their face in their hands. A figure approached cautiously, and

FUTURE looked up, eyes brimming with unshed tears. "I thought our visions could change the world," their voice cracked. "But all I see now is a shattered mosaic of what could've been."

In a desperate quest for affirmation, FUTURE sought solace in the company of someone equally damaged. The newcomer's words were like a siren's song, resonating with FUTURE's disillusionment. "They'll never understand you as I do," the newcomer whispered, cultivating a toxic bond. FUTURE's gaze lingered on them, a spark of dangerous hope igniting.

PRESENT's footsteps echoed through the park, their face etched with emotions. The playground, once filled with laughter, now stood deserted. In a moment of vulnerability, PRESENT sought refuge in a bustling café and poured the frustrations into a stranger, PRESENT's voice trembling. "I'm tired of being caught in the crossfire. It's like they don't even care how much this is tearing us apart."

The stranger leaned in, their expression empathetic. "You know, maybe it's time you prioritize yourself," they suggested. "You don't always have to be the peacekeeper."

The sun hung low in the sky, casting long shadows across the battered park. PAST had sought refuge on a bench near the entrance, FUTURE had found solace beneath a familiar tree, and PRESENT had been drawn to the heart of the park, the site of their countless discussions. It was here, amid the ruins of their once-harmonious friendship, that fate would bring them together.

PAST glanced up from contemplation as PRESENT approached, the weariness etched on their face evident even from a distance. PAST's voice was heavy with bitterness. They said, "Ah, the mediator. Have you come to try and rewrite history once again?"

PRESENT sighed, the weight of the role bearing down on them. "PAST, you know that's not my intention. We must find common ground, learn from you, and FUTURE."

Just as the tension began to thicken, FUTURE emerged from the shadows, showing an expression with a mixture of determination and frustration. "What good in learning from the past if we're forever bound by it?" FUTURE retorted, the optimism in their voice now tinged with sarcasm.

PAST's eyes narrowed and locked onto FUTURE, carrying a tone dripping with disdain. "So, you're still trying to convince us to discard everything we've learned?"

A tense silence settled over the trio. PAST stood steeped in history, FUTURE gazed ahead toward uncharted possibilities, and PRESENT, caught between them, struggled to bridge the chasm.

"Enough." PRESENT's voice broke the silence, a hint of desperation underlying their words. "We're all here now. Can't we find a way to honor the past while embracing change?"

FUTURE's laughter was bitter. "Honor history? Or cling to it as an excuse for stagnation?"

PAST's expression darkened, their retort dripping with scorn. "Change for the sake of change is the height of ignorance."

The sparks of argument ignited, the park once again echoing their heated words. PRESENT, with a heart heavy, stepped between the two, their voice a plea for reason. "Can't we see that there's merit in both perspectives? PAST, your lessons offer wisdom, and FUTURE, your visions bring hope."

But the flames of their disagreement were unrelenting. PAST turned away with a scoff, dismissing PRESENT's words. FUTURE's gaze remained stubbornly fixed on the horizon, an unspoken challenge to their counterparts.

CHAPTER 4

WAR

WAR

The tension between PAST, FUTURE, and PRESENT reached its boiling point, and the once-harmonious park became a battleground of clashing personalities. The ground trembled beneath their conflicting views, and the air was hostile.

PAST, with a furrowed brow and a deep sense of responsibility, recalled past mistakes and attempted to impose life lessons on their friends. It believed that understanding history was crucial to avoid the same pitfalls in the future. Their voice echoed with the wisdom of ages gone by, and they felt a duty to guide their friends away from repeating the errors of the past.

"Why can't they see the significance of the past? Trauma and abuse are cruel teachers, and I've learned the lessons the hard way. I carry the weight of our mistakes, and it's my responsibility to ensure they don't repeat those errors. They must understand the consequences of their actions and the decisions they make. My friends may not always appreciate my caution, but I can't bear to watch them stumble into the same traps that once ensnared me. If only they'd listen and learn from what's already happened, they might spare themselves the pain and turmoil that I've endured."

FUTURE, equally determined and with unwavering ambition, envisioned strategies to avoid past mistakes by dismissing PAST's cautionary tales. They felt that dwelling on yesterday was holding them back, and they were eager to charge into the future with unbridled optimism. Their eyes gleamed with the excitement of unexplored frontiers.

"Why is PAST so fixated on what's already done? The past is just that—a thing of the past. Dwelling on the trauma and abuse that shaped it is a waste of time. The real potential lies in the future, and I'm determined to reach it. There's so much to explore, so many possibilities to seize. I'm not afraid to take risks and push boundaries. My friends may think I'm reckless, but I'm driven by my vision for what's ahead. I refuse to let the scars of the past hold me back. The future is ours for the taking."

Caught in the middle, PRESENT darted between their friends, trying to keep the peace but imposing their belief that they were both wrong. They argued that they lived in idealized worlds, missing the most important aspect—the present. PRESENT wanted them to embrace the joys of the here and now and not be burdened by the past or constrained by the future.

"Why do they have to be so stubborn? Can't they see the value in balancing the past and the future with the present? I understand that the wisdom of the past is essential, and the excitement of the future is enticing. But they're missing the point—the here and now matters too. There's beauty in the moment, in the present experiences and connections. Life is fleeting, and we need to appreciate every second of it. I want them to embrace the joy of living in the present and cherish what's right in front of them without being burdened by regrets or ambition. If only they could find that balance, it'd be much easier for us all."

Their emotions spiraled out of control, and they hurled words at each other like weapons, their once-strong bond withering under the weight of ego and stubbornness.

"You're stuck in the past, refusing to see the potential of the future!" FUTURE accused, their voice sharp with frustration. "You keep carrying the weight of trauma and abuse as if they define you. But there's so much more to who you are and who you can become. Embrace the lessons without letting them imprison you. Don't let the shadows of yesterday overshadow the brilliance of tomorrow."

PAST's eyes flashed with indignation. "The trauma and abuse I've endured are not just burdens to be cast aside. They are part of my story, shaping the person I've become. Ignoring them would be a disservice to me and to others who have faced similar struggles. Acknowledging the past doesn't mean I'm stuck; it means I'm learning, growing, and using those experiences to build a better future."

PRESENT interjected, "Both of you are blind to the wonders of the present! We need to focus on what's happening right now! Let's not let our fixation on either extreme rob us of the richness of the present experience."

As the battle raged on, their egos seemed to fortify their positions, and the possibility of reconciliation became more distant with each passing moment.

In their pride, they failed to see that their differences were not weaknesses to overcome, but strengths that could complement each other. The beauty of their friendship was buried beneath the rubble of their discord, and it seemed that war was indeed inevitable.

With each passing argument, the bonds that had once woven them together grew weaker. Their garden, once a symbol of unity, withered under the stress of their discord. As PAST sat in quiet contemplation, a shadowy figure materialized nearby, and PAST's gaze locked onto the distant horizon. The presence seemed to carry an air of frustration, as if they bore the weight of unspoken anger. The figure's words held a certain edge, encouraging PAST to channel the pent-up emotions toward the present and the future.

"Look at them." The figure's words dripped with bitterness and resentment. "They wander through life oblivious to the pain we've endured. Their dreams are unfettered by the trauma and abuse that have marked our past." PAST felt a stirring within, a sense of solidarity with the figure's perspective. The wounds resonated with the figure's resentment, forming an unexpected connection.

FUTURE wandered the desolate park, hopeful eyes now clouded with despair. Beneath a canopy of trees, they sank to the ground, burying their face in their hands. A figure approached cautiously, and FUTURE looked up, eyes brimming with unshed tears. "I thought our visions could change the world," their voice cracked. "But all I see now is a shattered mosaic of what could've been."

In a desperate quest for affirmation, FUTURE sought solace in the company of someone equally damaged. The newcomer's words were like a siren's song, resonating with FUTURE's disillusionment. "They'll never understand you as I do," the newcomer whispered, cultivating a toxic bond. FUTURE's gaze lingered on them, a spark of dangerous hope igniting.

PRESENT's footsteps echoed through the park, their face etched with emotions. The playground, once filled with laughter, now stood deserted. In a moment of vulnerability, PRESENT sought refuge in a bustling café and poured the frustrations into a stranger, PRESENT's voice trembling. "I'm tired of being caught in the crossfire. It's like they don't even care how much this is tearing us apart."

The stranger leaned in, their expression empathetic. "You know, maybe it's time you prioritize yourself," they suggested. "You don't always have to be the peacekeeper."

The sun hung low in the sky, casting long shadows across the battered park. PAST had sought refuge on a bench near the entrance, FUTURE had found solace beneath a familiar tree, and PRESENT had been drawn to the heart of the park, the site of their countless discussions. It was here, amid the ruins of their once-harmonious friendship, that fate would bring them together.

PAST glanced up from contemplation as PRESENT approached, the weariness etched on their face evident even from a distance. PAST's voice was heavy with bitterness. They said, "Ah, the mediator. Have you come to try and rewrite history once again?"

PRESENT sighed, the weight of the role bearing down on them. "PAST, you know that's not my intention. We must find common ground, learn from you, and FUTURE."

Just as the tension began to thicken, FUTURE emerged from the shadows, showing an expression with a mixture of determination and frustration. "What good in learning from the past if we're forever bound by it?" FUTURE retorted, the optimism in their voice now tinged with sarcasm.

PAST's eyes narrowed and locked onto FUTURE, carrying a tone dripping with disdain. "So, you're still trying to convince us to discard everything we've learned?"

A tense silence settled over the trio. PAST stood steeped in history, FUTURE gazed ahead toward uncharted possibilities, and PRESENT, caught between them, struggled to bridge the chasm.

"Enough." PRESENT's voice broke the silence, a hint of desperation underlying their words. "We're all here now. Can't we find a way to honor the past while embracing change?"

FUTURE's laughter was bitter. "Honor history? Or cling to it as an excuse for stagnation?"

PAST's expression darkened, their retort dripping with scorn. "Change for the sake of change is the height of ignorance."

The sparks of argument ignited, the park once again echoing their heated words. PRESENT, with a heart heavy, stepped between the two, their voice a plea for reason. "Can't we see that there's merit in both perspectives? PAST, your lessons offer wisdom, and FUTURE, your visions bring hope."

But the flames of their disagreement were unrelenting. PAST turned away with a scoff, dismissing PRESENT's words. FUTURE's gaze remained stubbornly fixed on the horizon, an unspoken challenge to their counterparts.

PEACE

CHAPTER 4: PEACE

Amid the turmoil, a gentle voice broke through the cacophony. It was an old man, his name was *Wisdom*, sitting on a nearby bench, observing the heated exchange with a sense of wisdom and understanding. He had been a frequent visitor to the park, quietly observing the trio's friendship blossom over the years.

He slowly stood and approached the battling friends, his eyes full of compassion. "My dear friends," he said, his voice carrying a soothing tone, "I've watched you grow and share moments of joy and laughter here in this very park. Your friendship was once a beacon of hope for others. Do you not remember?"

PAST, FUTURE, and PRESENT turned their attention to the wise elder, momentarily distracted from their argument. "But we cannot agree on how to move forward," FUTURE retorted, frustration evident in their voice.

The old man smiled knowingly. "Ah, that is the beauty of true friendship. Differences will always exist, but it is in embracing those differences that you can create something extraordinary."

PAST looked skeptical but listened intently. "What do you mean?"

The old man gestured toward the oak tree towering above them. "That tree stands tall because it has deep roots in the past, and it stretches its branches toward the future. Just like your friendship, it should be grounded in the lessons of history and embrace the possibilities of tomorrow."

PRESENT's eyes lit up with realization, and they nodded in agreement. "You mean we can combine our strengths and learn from each other?"

"Exactly," the old man said warmly. "The past provides wisdom, the future offers vision, and the present, well, it keeps you anchored in the moment. Embrace these aspects within yourselves and work together, and you'll find a path that harmonizes your individual perspectives."

PAST and FUTURE exchanged glances, contemplating the elder's words. They had been so focused on proving their own viewpoints that they hadn't considered the power of collaboration.

PAST, FUTURE, and PRESENT stood on the battlefield of their shattered friendship, and a small flower from the once-vibrant garden caught their attention. It was a tiny symbol of resilience, bravely pushing through the hardened earth despite the harsh surroundings.

The flower's delicate petals were a stark contrast to the hostility that had consumed them. It served as a reminder of the beauty and strength that could emerge even in the darkest times. The sight of the flower struck a chord within each of them.

Realization slowly dawned upon PAST, FUTURE, and PRESENT. Despite the adversity surrounding it, they saw their reflection in the flower's unwavering determination to bloom. It was as if nature was offering them a profound lesson that they desperately needed to learn.

They looked at each other. Their eyes softened with newfound understanding. They saw the pain they had caused one another and recognized the preciousness of their friendship—the bond that had once held them together.

At that moment, they understood that their differences made them a formidable team, just as the past, future, and present are intertwined in life. Each brought something unique and valuable to their friendship, and their true strength lay in embracing these differences.

PAST spoke first, looking at FUTURE with a sense of understanding, "You know, I was so fixated on preserving the memories of the past that I failed to see the potential for growth and positive change in the future. Your vision is a gift, and I should have embraced it, not resisted it."

FUTURE smiled warmly, acknowledging PAST's words. "And I must admit, I often neglected the things that happened in the past. I was so caught up in the possibilities of what could be that I didn't fully appreciate the foundation we built together. Your wisdom and experience are invaluable to me."

With tears in their eyes, PRESENT added, "I'm sorry for imposing my beliefs on both of you and not understanding the value of your perspectives."

As they spoke, a sense of relief washed over them. They realized they were not enemies fighting against each other but friends who had lost their way. They were three unique individuals with distinct viewpoints, and that diversity was a gift they needed to cherish.

PAST said, "Imagine the wealth of knowledge we can gather from the past and the possibilities we can explore in the future. The present will serve as the bridge between the two, allowing us to make informed decisions and create a brighter tomorrow."

PRESENT smiled, "And in the present, we will cherish every moment, savoring the beauty of life and the connections we build with others. It is the present that binds us all, and we must cherish it as much as the past and the future."

FUTURE's gaze turned skyward, "Indeed, the future is vast and full of uncertainty, but it is also ripe with potential. Together, we shall forge our path, leaving behind a legacy that spans the ages."

Under the watchful eyes of the ancient oak tree, they made a silent promise—a pledge to embrace each other's strengths and learn from one another. They decided to work together, combining their perspectives and ideas to build a better future, just as they had built their garden together.

As they turned toward the garden, they saw the flowers responding to their reconciliation. The once-wilting blooms seemed to rise, and the colors intensified as if celebrating the return of harmony.

Their friendship, like the garden, needed tending and care. It would not always be easy, and they knew disagreements would still arise. But they also knew that they could overcome any obstacle with open hearts and a willingness to listen.

As they walked together, their bond grew stronger with each step, and they couldn't help but reflect on their past adventures and shared perspectives. PAST chuckled, reminiscing about an old escapade. "Do you remember that time we got lost in the ancient city? We were so disoriented, but somehow, we managed to find our way back together."

PRESENT grinned. "Oh, how could I forget! It felt like we were living in a history book, exploring the streets that held tales of centuries gone by. And FUTURE, you kept predicting what the city would become, and surprisingly, many of your visions came true!"

FUTURE nodded, a hint of nostalgia in their eyes. "That was a moment when we truly appreciated each other's unique gifts. PAST, your knowledge of history grounded us, and PRESENT, your enthusiasm made the journey even more exciting."

They continued to share stories and laughter, weaving together the tapestry of their friendship. As the night sky twinkled above them, PAST asked thoughtfully, "So, where do we go from here? What's the next adventure for us?"

FUTURE gazed at the stars, contemplating the question. "Our next adventure lies not just in the distant future but in the present, where we can make a difference right now. Let's continue connecting with people, bridging divides, and fostering understanding. There are still so many lives to touch, so many conflicts to resolve."

PRESENT nodded enthusiastically. "Absolutely! We should organize more gatherings that bring people together. Sharing our own journey of reconciliation might inspire others to take that crucial step toward peace."

PAST added, "And let's not forget the power of storytelling. Our own experiences have shaped us, but hearing stories from others can open hearts and minds like nothing else."

CHAPTER 5: UTOPIA

United once more, PAST, FUTURE, and PRESENT embarked on a remarkable journey, their friendship stronger and more harmonious than ever before. They understood that their perspectives were powerful when united, and together, they sought to create a utopia where the best of each era could coexist in harmony.

PAST, preserved all the valuable life lessons from the past, not just focusing on the faults but also cherishing the triumphs and achievements of humanity. PAST shared stories of resilience, compassion, and progress, reminding the community of their shared heritage and their potential to build upon it.

With their innovative and forward-thinking spirit, FUTURE became the architect of solutions for every conceivable scenario. They used the past as a foundation to create visionary plans for a sustainable and prosperous future. FUTURE worked tirelessly to ensure their utopia was resilient and prepared to face the challenges ahead. "Working with PAST has taught me the importance of finding balance and taking inspiration from what has come before."

PRESENT, the joyous and festive spirit, became the heart and soul of the utopia, fostering a sense of togetherness and celebration. They organized events and gatherings that brought people from all corners of the community together, nurturing a spirit of unity and understanding. PRESENT reminded everyone of the beauty of the present moment, encouraging them to savor life's simple pleasures and find joy in the everyday. "I used to think the present was all that mattered, but now I see the beauty in connecting the threads of time," PRESENT thought. "My role in nurturing unity and celebrating life is so much more meaningful when I understand the context provided by PAST and FUTURE."

In this utopia, individuals were encouraged to reflect on their past, long for their future, and cherish their present, all while understanding the importance of their interconnectedness. The community thrived as they embraced the wisdom of the past, the potential of the future, and the significance of the present.

The three friends convened regular gatherings under the shade of the ancient oak tree, inviting the community to share their stories and experiences. They listened with empathy and compassion, recognizing that each individual's journey was part of their utopia.

During one of these gatherings, an elder from the community stepped forward, her eyes filled with memories of a lifetime, and PAST welcomed her warmly, knowing that the stories of the elderly held immense wisdom and insights.

The elder began to speak. Her name was *Restoration*, her voice carrying the weight of history. "Long ago, this land was torn by strife and discord. Families feuded, and neighbors became enemies. We forgot the value of understanding and compassion, consumed by our differences."

PRESENT leaned in attentively. "But you found a way to overcome that, didn't you?"

Restoration nodded. "Indeed, young one. We were fortunate to have wise leaders who encouraged dialogue and unity. They reminded us that our shared humanity bound us despite our disagreements."

FUTURE said, "That's precisely what we aim for in this utopia—to embrace our differences while recognizing our common ground."

Restoration smiled. "It warms my heart to see the young generation taking up the mantle of unity. Your friendship sets a powerful example for us all."

As word of their extraordinary friendship spread, people from neighboring regions and even distant lands were drawn to their utopia. They sought solace, inspiration, and a sense of belonging, finding all of it within the warm embrace of PAST, FUTURE, and PRESENT's utopia.

Their garden, once a symbol of conflict, blossomed into a vibrant oasis of unity. The flowers from different eras intertwined, their colors blending harmoniously, just as the past, present, and future had united in friendship.

In this utopia, people found their true purpose and passion. They celebrated past achievements, pursued their dreams, and lived joyfully in the present. The community thrived, not because it was perfect, but because it embraced imperfections as opportunities for growth and learning.

As the years passed, the oak tree stood tall, its branches spreading wide like the outstretched arms of a guardian. Under its watchful gaze, PAST, FUTURE, and PRESENT continued inspiring generations with their timeless friendship.

Yet even in their idyllic haven, challenges emerged, shadows from the past returning to haunt them. A mysterious figure, a specter from their shared history, materialized with evil intent, threatening to unravel the very fabric of their utopia. PAST found themself paralyzed by the fear of a return to old wounds. Understanding the gravity of the situation, PRESENT and FUTURE joined forces to aid their friend.

PAST's voice was uncertain. "This figure reminds me of the past I'd rather forget. I fear it will undo all we've achieved."

The specter's presence served as a stark reminder to PAST, a haunting testament to the enduring grip of traumas. "PAST, recall your own words," the figure intoned, "the way they belittled your struggles, your upbringing, the cruelty the world showed you due to the past abuses. They could never truly grasp your pain."

Amid the haunting resonance of the figure's words, a shiver coursed through PAST's very being. The weight of their past, the scars of their experiences, seemed to converge in this moment, a suffocating fog of anguish. The figure's piercing gaze bore into PAST's soul, unraveling their defenses, and leaving them raw and exposed.

As the echoes of the figure's words reverberated, PAST's fear swelled, threatening to consume them entirely. The memories, once buried beneath layers of denial, surged forth with a vengeance. The pain of being misunderstood, the isolation of enduring silent battles, all seemed to resurface in an unrelenting torrent.

In that instant, PAST's yearning for escape from the memories grew overwhelming. With a voice quivering, PAST finally spoke, eyes cast down in a mix of vulnerability and desperation, "Can I . . . can I come with you? I want to leave it all behind, the pain, the memories. Please let me find refuge from this torment."

As PAST's trembling hand reached out to grasp the figure's, a sudden interruption shattered the moment. PRESENT, a dynamic force of the here and now, materialized beside PAST in a burst of urgency. With a firm yet gentle grip, PRESENT pulled PAST back from the precipice, a flash of concern in their eyes.

"Wait." PRESENT's voice cut through the longing and uncertainty. "Before you make this choice, remember what we've learned together. Remember that healing isn't about escaping your past, but about confronting it, understanding it, and finding resilience within yourself."

Startled, PAST turned to face PRESENT and FUTURE, caught between the figure's beckoning promise and the grounding presence of the present moment. The memories of their shared journey echoed in PAST's mind—the moments of growth, the strides toward self-awareness, and the hard-won progress in coming to terms with the pain of the past.

FUTURE's gaze held a mixture of care and determination. "I know the allure of escape is strong," they continued, "but true healing comes from facing your pain head-on. You've already come so far. Don't let the shadows of the past lead you astray now."

With a mixture of determination and gratitude, PAST withdrew their hand from the figure's reach and turned toward PRESENT. They acknowledged the lessons of their shared journey, the resilience they had gained, and the progress they had made.

"Thank you," PAST said, their voice steady despite the conflict within. "I choose to stay and confront my past, to continue growing and healing. It won't be easy, but I understand now that it's the path toward true liberation."

As the figure faded back into the shadows, and as PRESENT's reassuring presence lingered, PAST felt a renewed sense of purpose. The allure of escape had been tempting, but the wisdom of the present moment prevailed. With renewed determination, PAST embarked on the challenging yet ultimately rewarding journey of confronting their past, with the understanding that true healing could only be found through embracing the entirety of their experiences.

One afternoon, a merciless wildfire consumed the once-tranquil gardens, and panic and despair gripped PRESENT. They stood frozen, helpless amid the chaos, feeling the weight of their name, realizing that their essence was slipping through their fingers like grains of sand.

PAST reached out to PRESENT. "My friend, remember the trials we've overcome. Our past is rich with stories of resilience. We've extinguished fires before, and we'll do it again."

PRESENT's voice trembled, "But this . . . it's consuming everything so quickly. What can we do?"

FUTURE's voice said with determination, "We can overcome this, backed by the wisdom of the past and the innovation of the future. Remember, PAST's whispers can guide us to techniques that have worked in the past."

PAST's soothing cadence continued, "And combined with your determination, PRESENT, we can adapt those techniques and forge new strategies. FUTURE's foresight will illuminate the path ahead."

UNITED, they strategized. PAST's memories provided insights into fire containment methods, PRESENT's urgency spurred quick decision-making, and FUTURE's foresight guided their actions toward optimal outcomes.

"We'll create firebreaks, drawing from PAST's historical knowledge," PRESENT declared.

FUTURE interjected with a strategic edge. "We'll use controlled burns, simultaneously drawing from the past and planning for a safer future."

PAST's whisper was a steady reassurance. "And we'll work tirelessly, side by side, ensuring that this paradise is preserved."

In a synchronized dance of efforts, they fought the blaze. PAST's wisdom merged with FUTURE's ingenuity under PRESENT's timely execution. Flames were quenched, and order was gradually restored.

FUTURE's ability to travel in the future years granted it a unique perspective, but it also led to unintended consequences. They journeyed too far into the future, discovering a desolate world where PAST and PRESENT were absent.

When they finally returned to the embrace of PAST and PRESENT, they couldn't contain their sorrow.

"FUTURE, you look burdened," PAST observed gently. "What did you see?"

FUTURE's voice was tinged with melancholy. "I saw a world without the presence of both of you. Your absence had cast a shadow over everything. The people were lost without guidance."

PAST's voice carried wisdom and reassurance. "Remember, FUTURE, that our past has taught us that change is possible. The future is shaped by the choices we make today. Our presence and actions can create a different destiny."

PRESENT, their essence a calming embrace, added, "FUTURE, the world we saw was a reminder of the importance of the present. We can avoid such a future by focusing on fostering our bond and unity."

FUTURE, though heavy-hearted, found solace in their words. "You're right," they admitted, "our unity is our strength. The bonds we nurture in the present can influence the future."

In their united front, they faced this new challenge head-on, determined to prevent the bleak future that FUTURE had witnessed. They began by strengthening their friendship, learning from the past, and applying those lessons to their current endeavors.

CHAPTER 6: SYMPOSIUM

The air buzzed with electric anticipation in the heart of an elegant symposium hall. At the forefront stood three enigmatic figures—PAST, PRESENT, and FUTURE—each exuding an aura that resonated with their temporal essence. The symposium was a gathering of minds transcending time, exploring human experience through past, present, and future dimensions.

PAST initiated the dialogue. "Welcome, dear participants, to this convergence of time. As we delve into the stories that shape us, share a memory from your past—a memory that still lingers as a wound, a lesson, or a shadow."

Voices from the audience, rich with emotion, recounted stories of regret, loss, and pivotal moments. Amid them, a voice rose, trembling yet resolute. "I remember when I let go of something I loved dearly, convinced that it was the right choice. But as the years passed, I realized the gravity of that decision and the irreplaceable void it left. It's a memory I can't shake."

Another attendee with a sad voice chimed in, "I can relate to that more than you know. I once walked away from a once-in-a-lifetime opportunity because I feared its uncertainty. Every time I see someone else seize such a chance, I'm haunted by what might have been."

A man with a weathered face and a distant gaze spoke up, his voice heavy with regret, "I lost the trust of someone I cherished deeply. My actions at the time seemed justified, but in hindsight, they were a terrible mistake. It's a lesson I've learned too late and plagues me daily."

A hushed whisper from an elderly woman in the back added, "I held back my true feelings, convinced there would always be time to express them. But then life showed me its unpredictable side, and the person I loved was taken away too soon. The words I never said still echo in my heart."

PAST nodded, an understanding glint in their eyes. This monologue was a reminder that the past held moments of triumph and scars, each influencing the journey forward.

Amid these confessions, a voice of compassion and understanding rose. "We all carry the weight of our decisions, the what-ifs, and the could-have-beens. But let this gathering remind us that we are not alone in our regrets. By sharing our stories, we offer each other solace and a chance to heal."

PRESENT, vibrant and captivating, took the spotlight next. "In this precise moment, let go of distractions and tune in to your current reality. What's happening in your life right now? Share your joys, your fears, and your aspirations."

Laughter and contemplative murmurs filled the room as participants shared snippets of their present lives—achievements, challenges, mundane joys. Amid them, a voice emerged, tinged with anxiety. "I find myself lost in future thoughts, drowning in what-ifs and worries. The more I try to control the outcome, the more it slips away."

PRESENT listened attentively, an empathetic nod acknowledging the struggle. This echoed a universal sentiment—the challenge of staying anchored to the present amid the pull of the unknown.

"Life is a mosaic of moments—some challenging, some joyful. By focusing on the present, we can find a sense of balance amid the chaos. It's about acknowledging the past, planning for the future, but most importantly, living fully in the now."

Finally, FUTURE, an embodiment of anticipation, stepped into the limelight. "Picture a future where your fears have faded, and your ambitions have blossomed into reality. What does that future hold for you? And what steps can you take today to inch closer to that vision?"

Dreams and ambitions flowed from the audience, mingled with uncertainties about the path ahead. Among them, a voice rang out, trembling yet determined. "The future terrifies me. The sheer magnitude of its uncertainty overwhelms my thoughts. What if I make the wrong choices? What if I end up alone?"

A woman with a warm smile shared, "I used to be afraid of change, of stepping into the unknown. But as I faced challenges and embraced new opportunities, I realized that growth often comes from pushing past our comfort zones."

A man with a hint of nostalgia said, "Looking back, some of my best experiences were the ones I never saw coming. The future might hold surprises—some challenging, some delightful. Embracing them with an open heart can lead to unexpected joy."

A voice filled with determination added, "I've started getting small, achievable goals for myself. They help me focus on the present while giving me a direction for the future. It's like building stepping stones toward my vision."

A young person with a fire in their eyes shared, "I've decided to pursue my passion, even though it might not be the most conventional path. The future may hold uncertainties, but I'd rather take risks and create my path than regret not trying."

FUTURE's gaze held a comforting assurance. This monologue was a testament to the fragility of human hopes, yet it revealed the strength borne from acknowledging fears and taking gradual steps toward a brighter horizon.

Amid these discussions, a voice of encouragement resonated. "The future can indeed be daunting, but it's also a canvas of endless possibilities. By acknowledging your fears and taking small steps forward, you're already shaping the narrative of what's to come."

The three panelists convened as the symposium reached its zenith. They collectively addressed the audience, uniting the lines of time in a profound synthesis.

PAST reminds us to honor our history, as it is the foundation upon which we stand. PRESENT urges us to embrace the current moment, for it is where life unfolds. FUTURE encourages us to channel our aspirations into meaningful actions, sculpting the destiny we envision."

The audience, stirred by this harmonious blend of insights, felt a renewed sense of purpose. The individual who had expressed anxieties about the future now saw a path illuminated with hope. Others recognized the importance of shedding the shackles of the past to engage with the present fully.

The symposium drew to a close, but its impact lingered in the hearts and minds of all who had attended. PAST, PRESENT, and FUTURE, like guiding stars, illuminated the depths of human experience. As the attendees left the hall, they carried a newfound understanding of the symphony of time that resonated with their past, harmonized with their present, and composed the melody of their future.

CHAPTER 7: WORKSHOP

In the workshop, a group of individuals transitioned from the symposium to engage with TENSES—representing the PAST, PRESENT, and FUTURE—in a collaborative endeavor to unravel the intricacies of tenses and gain a profound comprehension of their life experiences.

As the participants settled into the workshop space, PAST stepped forward, their voice carrying the weight of history and memory. PAST began, "I invite you to consider a question: *What stands out to you the most about our story?* Take a moment to reflect upon the chapters of your life that have shaped you, the moments that have left unforgettable imprints upon your heart and mind."

The room grew quiet as each participant allowed the question to sink in. Memories flickered, anecdotes surfaced, and emotions stirred. This question urged them to journey into the past and uncover the gems illuminating the path they had trodden thus far. It was the starting point of their exploration, a thread that would guide them through the intricate narrative of their existence.

After a contemplative pause, the embodiment of PRESENT stepped forward, their presence vibrant and immediate. "Building upon the threads of our story," PRESENT began, reflecting on this question: *Which of us do you identify with most?* "It explores the tapestry of time that resonates most profoundly within your being. Are you anchored in the lessons of PAST, fully immersed in the energy of PRESENT, or driven by the direction of FUTURE?"

The essence of each tense tugged at their consciousness, beckoning them to introspect and understand their inclinations. Some found themselves drawn to the stability of the PAST, others felt the magnetic pull of the PRESENT, living fully in the now and savoring its immediacy. And then there were those whose gaze was fixed upon the horizon of the FUTURE, where possibilities beckoned.

With the resonance of the previous question still lingering in the air, the embodiment of FUTURE stepped forward. FUTURE's voice carried a sense of wonder. "Consider this question: *Up to this point in your life, who have been the most influential people and what tenses do you think they tend to live in most?*"

FUTURE's question unveiled a new layer of inquiry, prompting them to not only think of the people who had left a memorable mark but also to consider the temporal dimensions in which these individuals resided. Did the influential figures of their lives live predominantly in the PAST, drawing wisdom from history? Were they firmly rooted in the PRESENT, embracing every moment with intensity? Or were they dreamers of the FUTURE, inspiring with their vision and aspirations?

While the echoes of the previous contemplations still resonated, PAST's voice held both empathy and understanding. "Let us explore a question that invites introspection: *Which of us tenses cause you the most pain?* Confronting discomfort is essential for growth, and in acknowledging the tense that evokes pain, you embark on a path of healing."

It was a moment of vulnerability as each person coped with the painful memories or regrets that tethered them to the past. For some, it was the sting of missed opportunities and unfulfilled hopes. For others, it was the haunting specter of past mistakes. And yet, some found their pain rooted in the uncertainty of the future, the fear of the unknown.

PRESENT spoke, their presence pulsating with strength. PRESENT's voice carried a sense of immediacy. "*When the three of us fight in your life, who usually wins?* This delves into the heart of your inner conflicts, revealing the prevailing tense that holds sway during moments of turmoil."

It was a challenge to uncover the dominant tense during times of internal struggle. They recognized the PAST's ability to cast shadows of doubt; some people thought PRESENT's urgency took precedence and some felt the weight of the FUTURE's uncertainties. The battle between these tenses reflected their inner conflicts, each tense vying for dominance.

With the wisdom from the previous discussions lingering in the air, PAST, PRESENT, and FUTURE stood united. "As we stand at the crossroads of our journey," their voices harmonized, "*Which of us is causing you the biggest problems right now, and what do you think you need to do about it?*"

Participants were seeking to identify the tense that holds the most significant influence over their current challenges. Some were burdened with the ghosts of the PAST, struggling to break free from past mistakes. Others were weighed down by the frantic demands of the PRESENT, leaving them overwhelmed and drained. And then there were those whose apprehensions about the FUTURE stifled their growth.

With the collective reflections from the previous questions, PAST, PRESENT, and FUTURE gathered together. "*What inspiration or encouragement have you gained from the chapters of our lives called peace and utopia?* It invites you to seek wisdom from moments when our tenses merged in harmony."

It was an opportunity to draw from the serene moments of the PAST, the moments of presence and fulfillment from the PRESENT, and the visions of the FUTURE. They recalled instances when the tenses intertwined seamlessly, offering a glimpse of the peace and utopia that could be achieved within themselves.

With the culmination of the workshop's exploration drawing near, PAST, PRESENT, and FUTURE exuded an air of collective understanding. Their voices resonated in unison. "We offer a final question: *How else can we help you?* This extends an open hand, an opportunity for you to seek further guidance and support from PAST, PRESENT, and FUTURE personifications."

In response to this question, participants shared their thoughts and concerns. Some sought guidance on navigating challenging situations rooted in the past, while others sought strategies for living more fully in the present. Some yearned for insights on setting meaningful goals for the future. The room transformed into a sanctuary of introspection as attendees embraced the wisdom and perspectives offered by the tenses.

As the workshop drew close, participants departed with a renewed sense of connection to the tenses that shape their lives. PAST, PRESENT, and FUTURE personifications had served as guides through the intricate web of time, helping them understand the interplay of their lives' chapters. Armed with newfound insights, they walked away leading to a more balanced, mindful, and purposeful journey ahead.

CHAPTER 5

PEACE

Amid the turmoil, a gentle voice broke through the cacophony. It was an old man, his name was *Wisdom*, sitting on a nearby bench, observing the heated exchange with a sense of wisdom and understanding. He had been a frequent visitor to the park, quietly observing the trio's friendship blossom over the years.

He slowly stood and approached the battling friends, his eyes full of compassion. "My dear friends," he said, his voice carrying a soothing tone, "I've watched you grow and share moments of joy and laughter here in this very park. Your friendship was once a beacon of hope for others. Do you not remember?"

PAST, FUTURE, and PRESENT turned their attention to the wise elder, momentarily distracted from their argument. "But we cannot agree on how to move forward," FUTURE retorted, frustration evident in their voice.

The old man smiled knowingly. "Ah, that is the beauty of true friendship. Differences will always exist, but it is in embracing those differences that you can create something extraordinary."

PAST looked skeptical but listened intently. "What do you mean?"

The old man gestured toward the oak tree towering above them. "That tree stands tall because it has deep roots in the past, and it stretches its branches toward the future. Just like your friendship, it should be grounded in the lessons of history and embrace the possibilities of tomorrow."

PRESENT's eyes lit up with realization, and they nodded in agreement. "You mean we can combine our strengths and learn from each other?"

"Exactly," the old man said warmly. "The past provides wisdom, the future offers vision, and the present, well, it keeps you anchored in the moment. Embrace these aspects within yourselves and work together, and you'll find a path that harmonizes your individual perspectives."

PAST and FUTURE exchanged glances, contemplating the elder's words. They had been so focused on proving their own viewpoints that they hadn't considered the power of collaboration.

PAST, FUTURE, and PRESENT stood on the battlefield of their shattered friendship, and a small flower from the once-vibrant garden caught their attention. It was a tiny symbol of resilience, bravely pushing through the hardened earth despite the harsh surroundings.

The flower's delicate petals were a stark contrast to the hostility that had consumed them. It served as a reminder of the beauty and strength that could emerge even in the darkest times. The sight of the flower struck a chord within each of them.

Realization slowly dawned upon PAST, FUTURE, and PRESENT. Despite the adversity surrounding it, they saw their reflection in the flower's unwavering determination to bloom. It was as if nature was offering them a profound lesson that they desperately needed to learn.

They looked at each other. Their eyes softened with newfound understanding. They saw the pain they had caused one another and recognized the preciousness of their friendship—the bond that had once held them together.

At that moment, they understood that their differences made them a formidable team, just as the past, future, and present are intertwined in life. Each brought something unique and valuable to their friendship, and their true strength lay in embracing these differences.

PAST spoke first, looking at FUTURE with a sense of understanding, "You know, I was so fixated on preserving the memories of the past that I failed to see the potential for growth and positive change in the future. Your vision is a gift, and I should have embraced it, not resisted it."

FUTURE smiled warmly, acknowledging PAST's words. "And I must admit, I often neglected the things that happened in the past. I was so caught up in the possibilities of what could be that I didn't fully appreciate the foundation we built together. Your wisdom and experience are invaluable to me."

With tears in their eyes, PRESENT added, "I'm sorry for imposing my beliefs on both of you and not understanding the value of your perspectives."

As they spoke, a sense of relief washed over them. They realized they were not enemies fighting against each other but friends who had lost their way. They were three unique individuals with distinct viewpoints, and that diversity was a gift they needed to cherish.

PAST said, "Imagine the wealth of knowledge we can gather from the past and the possibilities we can explore in the future. The present will serve as the bridge between the two, allowing us to make informed decisions and create a brighter tomorrow."

PRESENT smiled, "And in the present, we will cherish every moment, savoring the beauty of life and the connections we build with others. It is the present that binds us all, and we must cherish it as much as the past and the future."

FUTURE's gaze turned skyward, "Indeed, the future is vast and full of uncertainty, but it is also ripe with potential. Together, we shall forge our path, leaving behind a legacy that spans the ages."

Under the watchful eyes of the ancient oak tree, they made a silent promise—a pledge to embrace each other's strengths and learn from one another. They decided to work together, combining their perspectives and ideas to build a better future, just as they had built their garden together.

As they turned toward the garden, they saw the flowers responding to their reconciliation. The once-wilting blooms seemed to rise, and the colors intensified as if celebrating the return of harmony.

Their friendship, like the garden, needed tending and care. It would not always be easy, and they knew disagreements would still arise. But they also knew that they could overcome any obstacle with open hearts and a willingness to listen.

As they walked together, their bond grew stronger with each step, and they couldn't help but reflect on their past adventures and shared perspectives. PAST chuckled, reminiscing about an old escapade. "Do you remember that time we got lost in the ancient city? We were so disoriented, but somehow, we managed to find our way back together."

PRESENT grinned. "Oh, how could I forget! It felt like we were living in a history book, exploring the streets that held tales of centuries gone by. And FUTURE, you kept predicting what the city would become, and surprisingly, many of your visions came true!"

FUTURE nodded, a hint of nostalgia in their eyes. "That was a moment when we truly appreciated each other's unique gifts. PAST, your knowledge of history grounded us, and PRESENT, your enthusiasm made the journey even more exciting."

They continued to share stories and laughter, weaving together the tapestry of their friendship. As the night sky twinkled above them, PAST asked thoughtfully, "So, where do we go from here? What's the next adventure for us?"

FUTURE gazed at the stars, contemplating the question. "Our next adventure lies not just in the distant future but in the present, where we can make a difference right now. Let's continue connecting with people, bridging divides, and fostering understanding. There are still so many lives to touch, so many conflicts to resolve."

PRESENT nodded enthusiastically. "Absolutely! We should organize more gatherings that bring people together. Sharing our own journey of reconciliation might inspire others to take that crucial step toward peace."

PAST added, "And let's not forget the power of storytelling. Our own experiences have shaped us, but hearing stories from others can open hearts and minds like nothing else."

CHAPTER 6

UTOPIA

United once more, PAST, FUTURE, and PRESENT embarked on a remarkable journey, their friendship stronger and more harmonious than ever before. They understood that their perspectives were powerful when united, and together, they sought to create a utopia where the best of each era could coexist in harmony.

PAST, preserved all the valuable life lessons from the past, not just focusing on the faults but also cherishing the triumphs and achievements of humanity. PAST shared stories of resilience, compassion, and progress, reminding the community of their shared heritage and their potential to build upon it.

With their innovative and forward-thinking spirit, FUTURE became the architect of solutions for every conceivable scenario. They used the past as a foundation to create visionary plans for a sustainable and prosperous future. FUTURE worked tirelessly to ensure their utopia was resilient and prepared to face the challenges ahead. "Working with PAST has taught me the importance of finding balance and taking inspiration from what has come before."

PRESENT, the joyous and festive spirit, became the heart and soul of the utopia, fostering a sense of togetherness and celebration. They organized events and gatherings that brought people from all corners of the community together, nurturing a spirit of unity and understanding. PRESENT reminded everyone of the beauty of the present moment, encouraging them to savor life's simple pleasures and find joy in the everyday. "I used to think the present was all that mattered, but now I see the beauty in connecting the threads of time," PRESENT thought. "My role in nurturing unity and celebrating life is so much more meaningful when I understand the context provided by PAST and FUTURE."

In this utopia, individuals were encouraged to reflect on their past, long for their future, and cherish their present, all while understanding the importance of their interconnectedness. The community thrived as they embraced the wisdom of the past, the potential of the future, and the significance of the present.

The three friends convened regular gatherings under the shade of the ancient oak tree, inviting the community to share their stories and experiences. They listened with empathy and compassion, recognizing that each individual's journey was part of their utopia.

During one of these gatherings, an elder from the community stepped forward, her eyes filled with memories of a lifetime, and PAST welcomed her warmly, knowing that the stories of the elderly held immense wisdom and insights.

The elder began to speak. Her name was *Restoration*, her voice carrying the weight of history. "Long ago, this land was torn by strife and discord. Families feuded, and neighbors became enemies. We forgot the value of understanding and compassion, consumed by our differences."

PRESENT leaned in attentively. "But you found a way to overcome that, didn't you?"

Restoration nodded. "Indeed, young one. We were fortunate to have wise leaders who encouraged dialogue and unity. They reminded us that our shared humanity bound us despite our disagreements."

FUTURE said, "That's precisely what we aim for in this utopia—to embrace our differences while recognizing our common ground."

Restoration smiled. "It warms my heart to see the young generation taking up the mantle of unity. Your friendship sets a powerful example for us all."

As word of their extraordinary friendship spread, people from neighboring regions and even distant lands were drawn to their utopia. They sought solace, inspiration, and a sense of belonging, finding all of it within the warm embrace of PAST, FUTURE, and PRESENT's utopia.

Their garden, once a symbol of conflict, blossomed into a vibrant oasis of unity. The flowers from different eras intertwined, their colors blending harmoniously, just as the past, present, and future had united in friendship.

In this utopia, people found their true purpose and passion. They celebrated past achievements, pursued their dreams, and lived joyfully in the present. The community thrived, not because it was perfect, but because it embraced imperfections as opportunities for growth and learning.

As the years passed, the oak tree stood tall, its branches spreading wide like the outstretched arms of a guardian. Under its watchful gaze, PAST, FUTURE, and PRESENT continued inspiring generations with their timeless friendship.

Yet even in their idyllic haven, challenges emerged, shadows from the past returning to haunt them. A mysterious figure, a specter from their shared history, materialized with evil intent, threatening to unravel the very fabric of their utopia. PAST found themself paralyzed by the fear of a return to old wounds. Understanding the gravity of the situation, PRESENT and FUTURE joined forces to aid their friend.

PAST's voice was uncertain. "This figure reminds me of the past I'd rather forget. I fear it will undo all we've achieved."

The specter's presence served as a stark reminder to PAST, a haunting testament to the enduring grip of traumas. "PAST, recall your own words," the figure intoned, "the way they belittled your struggles, your upbringing, the cruelty the world showed you due to the past abuses. They could never truly grasp your pain."

Amid the haunting resonance of the figure's words, a shiver coursed through PAST's very being. The weight of their past, the scars of their experiences, seemed to converge in this moment, a suffocating fog of anguish. The figure's piercing gaze bore into PAST's soul, unraveling their defenses, and leaving them raw and exposed.

As the echoes of the figure's words reverberated, PAST's fear swelled, threatening to consume them entirely. The memories, once buried beneath layers of denial, surged forth with a vengeance. The pain of being misunderstood, the isolation of enduring silent battles, all seemed to resurface in an unrelenting torrent.

In that instant, PAST's yearning for escape from the memories grew overwhelming. With a voice quivering, PAST finally spoke, eyes cast down in a mix of vulnerability and desperation, "Can I . . . can I come with you? I want to leave it all behind, the pain, the memories. Please let me find refuge from this torment."

As PAST's trembling hand reached out to grasp the figure's, a sudden interruption shattered the moment. PRESENT, a dynamic force of the here and now, materialized beside PAST in a burst of urgency. With a firm yet gentle grip, PRESENT pulled PAST back from the precipice, a flash of concern in their eyes.

"Wait." PRESENT's voice cut through the longing and uncertainty. "Before you make this choice, remember what we've learned together. Remember that healing isn't about escaping your past, but about confronting it, understanding it, and finding resilience within yourself."

Startled, PAST turned to face PRESENT and FUTURE, caught between the figure's beckoning promise and the grounding presence of the present moment. The memories of their shared journey echoed in PAST's mind—the moments of growth, the strides toward self-awareness, and the hard-won progress in coming to terms with the pain of the past.

FUTURE's gaze held a mixture of care and determination. "I know the allure of escape is strong," they continued, "but true healing comes from facing your pain head-on. You've already come so far. Don't let the shadows of the past lead you astray now."

With a mixture of determination and gratitude, PAST withdrew their hand from the figure's reach and turned toward PRESENT. They acknowledged the lessons of their shared journey, the resilience they had gained, and the progress they had made.

"Thank you," PAST said, their voice steady despite the conflict within. "I choose to stay and confront my past, to continue growing and healing. It won't be easy, but I understand now that it's the path toward true liberation."

As the figure faded back into the shadows, and as PRESENT's reassuring presence lingered, PAST felt a renewed sense of purpose. The allure of escape had been tempting, but the wisdom of the present moment prevailed. With renewed determination, PAST embarked on the challenging yet ultimately rewarding journey of confronting their past, with the understanding that true healing could only be found through embracing the entirety of their experiences.

One afternoon, a merciless wildfire consumed the once-tranquil gardens, and panic and despair gripped PRESENT. They stood frozen, helpless amid the chaos, feeling the weight of their name, realizing that their essence was slipping through their fingers like grains of sand.

PAST reached out to PRESENT. "My friend, remember the trials we've overcome. Our past is rich with stories of resilience. We've extinguished fires before, and we'll do it again."

PRESENT's voice trembled, "But this . . . it's consuming everything so quickly. What can we do?"

FUTURE's voice said with determination, "We can overcome this, backed by the wisdom of the past and the innovation of the future. Remember, PAST's whispers can guide us to techniques that have worked in the past."

PAST's soothing cadence continued, "And combined with your determination, PRESENT, we can adapt those techniques and forge new strategies. FUTURE's foresight will illuminate the path ahead."

UNITED, they strategized. PAST's memories provided insights into fire containment methods, PRESENT's urgency spurred quick decision-making, and FUTURE's foresight guided their actions toward optimal outcomes.

"We'll create firebreaks, drawing from PAST's historical knowledge," PRESENT declared.

FUTURE interjected with a strategic edge. "We'll use controlled burns, simultaneously drawing from the past and planning for a safer future."

PAST's whisper was a steady reassurance. "And we'll work tirelessly, side by side, ensuring that this paradise is preserved."

In a synchronized dance of efforts, they fought the blaze. PAST's wisdom merged with FUTURE's ingenuity under PRESENT's timely execution. Flames were quenched, and order was gradually restored.

FUTURE's ability to travel in the future years granted it a unique perspective, but it also led to unintended consequences. They journeyed too far into the future, discovering a desolate world where PAST and PRESENT were absent.

When they finally returned to the embrace of PAST and PRESENT, they couldn't contain their sorrow.

"FUTURE, you look burdened," PAST observed gently. "What did you see?"

FUTURE's voice was tinged with melancholy. "I saw a world without the presence of both of you. Your absence had cast a shadow over everything. The people were lost without guidance."

PAST's voice carried wisdom and reassurance. "Remember, FUTURE, that our past has taught us that change is possible. The future is shaped by the choices we make today. Our presence and actions can create a different destiny."

PRESENT, their essence a calming embrace, added, "FUTURE, the world we saw was a reminder of the importance of the present. We can avoid such a future by focusing on fostering our bond and unity."

FUTURE, though heavy-hearted, found solace in their words. "You're right," they admitted, "our unity is our strength. The bonds we nurture in the present can influence the future."

In their united front, they faced this new challenge head-on, determined to prevent the bleak future that FUTURE had witnessed.

They began by strengthening their friendship, learning from the past, and applying those lessons to their current endeavors.

CHAPTER 7

SYMPOSIUM

The air buzzed with electric anticipation in the heart of an elegant symposium hall. At the forefront stood three enigmatic figures—PAST, PRESENT, and FUTURE—each exuding an aura that resonated with their temporal essence. The symposium was a gathering of minds transcending time, exploring human experience through past, present, and future dimensions.

PAST initiated the dialogue. "Welcome, dear participants, to this convergence of time. As we delve into the stories that shape us, share a memory from your past—a memory that still lingers as a wound, a lesson, or a shadow."

Voices from the audience, rich with emotion, recounted stories of regret, loss, and pivotal moments. Amid them, a voice rose, trembling yet resolute. "I remember when I let go of something I loved dearly, convinced that it was the right choice. But as the years passed, I realized the gravity of that decision and the irreplaceable void it left. It's a memory I can't shake."

Another attendee with a sad voice chimed in, "I can relate to that more than you know. I once walked away from a once-in-a-lifetime opportunity because I feared its uncertainty. Every time I see someone else seize such a chance, I'm haunted by what might have been."

A man with a weathered face and a distant gaze spoke up, his voice heavy with regret, "I lost the trust of someone I cherished deeply. My actions at the time seemed justified, but in hindsight, they were a terrible mistake. It's a lesson I've learned too late and plagues me daily."

A hushed whisper from an elderly woman in the back added, "I held back my true feelings, convinced there would always be time to express them. But then life showed me its unpredictable side, and the person I loved was taken away too soon. The words I never said still echo in my heart."

PAST nodded, an understanding glint in their eyes. This monologue was a reminder that the past held moments of triumph and scars, each influencing the journey forward.

Amid these confessions, a voice of compassion and understanding rose. "We all carry the weight of our decisions, the what-ifs, and the could-have-beens. But let this gathering remind us that we are not alone in our regrets. By sharing our stories, we offer each other solace and a chance to heal."

PRESENT, vibrant and captivating, took the spotlight next. "In this precise moment, let go of distractions and tune in to your current reality. What's happening in your life right now? Share your joys, your fears, and your aspirations."

Laughter and contemplative murmurs filled the room as participants shared snippets of their present lives—achievements, challenges, mundane joys. Amid them, a voice emerged, tinged with anxiety. "I find myself lost in future thoughts, drowning in what-ifs and worries. The more I try to control the outcome, the more it slips away."

PRESENT listened attentively, an empathetic nod acknowledging the struggle. This echoed a universal sentiment—the challenge of staying anchored to the present amid the pull of the unknown.

"Life is a mosaic of moments—some challenging, some joyful. By focusing on the present, we can find a sense of balance amid the chaos. It's about acknowledging the past, planning for the future, but most importantly, living fully in the now."

Finally, FUTURE, an embodiment of anticipation, stepped into the limelight. "Picture a future where your fears have faded, and your ambitions have blossomed into reality. What does that future hold for you? And what steps can you take today to inch closer to that vision?"

Dreams and ambitions flowed from the audience, mingled with uncertainties about the path ahead. Among them, a voice rang out, trembling yet determined. "The future terrifies me. The sheer magnitude of its uncertainty overwhelms my thoughts. What if I make the wrong choices? What if I end up alone?"

A woman with a warm smile shared, "I used to be afraid of change, of stepping into the unknown. But as I faced challenges and embraced new opportunities, I realized that growth often comes from pushing past our comfort zones."

A man with a hint of nostalgia said, "Looking back, some of my best experiences were the ones I never saw coming. The future might hold surprises—some challenging, some delightful. Embracing them with an open heart can lead to unexpected joy."

A voice filled with determination added, "I've started getting small, achievable goals for myself. They help me focus on the present while giving me a direction for the future. It's like building stepping stones toward my vision."

A young person with a fire in their eyes shared, "I've decided to pursue my passion, even though it might not be the most conventional path. The future may hold uncertainties, but I'd rather take risks and create my path than regret not trying."

FUTURE's gaze held a comforting assurance. This monologue was a testament to the fragility of human hopes, yet it revealed the strength borne from acknowledging fears and taking gradual steps toward a brighter horizon.

Amid these discussions, a voice of encouragement resonated. "The future can indeed be daunting, but it's also a canvas of endless possibilities. By acknowledging your fears and taking small steps forward, you're already shaping the narrative of what's to come."

The three panelists convened as the symposium reached its zenith. They collectively addressed the audience, uniting the lines of time in a profound synthesis.

PAST reminds us to honor our history, as it is the foundation upon which we stand. PRESENT urges us to embrace the current moment, for it is where life unfolds. FUTURE encourages us to channel our aspirations into meaningful actions, sculpting the destiny we envision."

The audience, stirred by this harmonious blend of insights, felt a renewed sense of purpose. The individual who had expressed anxieties about the future now saw a path illuminated with hope. Others recognized the importance of shedding the shackles of the past to engage with the present fully.

The symposium drew to a close, but its impact lingered in the hearts and minds of all who had attended. PAST, PRESENT, and FUTURE, like guiding stars, illuminated the depths of human experience. As the attendees left the hall, they carried a newfound understanding of the symphony of time that resonated with their past, harmonized with their present, and composed the melody of their future.

CHAPTER 8

WORKSHOP

In the workshop, a group of individuals transitioned from the symposium to engage with TENSES—representing the PAST, PRESENT, and FUTURE—in a collaborative endeavor to unravel the intricacies of tenses and gain a profound comprehension of their life experiences.

As the participants settled into the workshop space, PAST stepped forward, their voice carrying the weight of history and memory. PAST began, "I invite you to consider a question: *What stands out to you the most about our story?* Take a moment to reflect upon the chapters of your life that have shaped you, the moments that have left unforgettable imprints upon your heart and mind."

The room grew quiet as each participant allowed the question to sink in. Memories flickered, anecdotes surfaced, and emotions stirred. This question urged them to journey into the past and uncover the gems illuminating the path they had trodden thus far. It was the starting point of their exploration, a thread that would guide them through the intricate narrative of their existence.

After a contemplative pause, the embodiment of PRESENT stepped forward, their presence vibrant and immediate. "Building upon the threads of our story," PRESENT began, reflecting on this question: *Which of us do you identify with most?* "It explores the tapestry of time that resonates most profoundly within your being. Are you anchored in the lessons of PAST, fully immersed in the energy of PRESENT, or driven by the direction of FUTURE?"

The essence of each tense tugged at their consciousness, beckoning them to introspect and understand their inclinations. Some found themselves drawn to the stability of the PAST, others felt the magnetic pull of the PRESENT, living fully in the now and savoring its immediacy. And then there were those whose gaze was fixed upon the horizon of the FUTURE, where possibilities beckoned.

With the resonance of the previous question still lingering in the air, the embodiment of FUTURE stepped forward. FUTURE's voice carried a sense of wonder. "Consider this question: *Up to this point in your life, who have been the most influential people and what tenses do you think they tend to live in most?*"

FUTURE's question unveiled a new layer of inquiry, prompting them to not only think of the people who had left a memorable mark but also to consider the temporal dimensions in which these individuals resided. Did the influential figures of their lives live predominantly in the PAST, drawing wisdom from history? Were they firmly rooted in the PRESENT, embracing every moment with intensity? Or were they dreamers of the FUTURE, inspiring with their vision and aspirations?

While the echoes of the previous contemplations still resonated, PAST's voice held both empathy and understanding. "Let us explore a question that invites introspection: *Which of us tenses cause you the most pain?* Confronting discomfort is essential for growth, and in acknowledging the tense that evokes pain, you embark on a path of healing."

It was a moment of vulnerability as each person coped with the painful memories or regrets that tethered them to the past. For some, it was the sting of missed opportunities and unfulfilled hopes. For others, it was the haunting specter of past mistakes. And yet, some found their pain rooted in the uncertainty of the future, the fear of the unknown.

PRESENT spoke, their presence pulsating with strength. PRESENT's voice carried a sense of immediacy. "*When the three of us fight in your life, who usually wins?* This delves into the heart of your inner conflicts, revealing the prevailing tense that holds sway during moments of turmoil."

It was a challenge to uncover the dominant tense during times of internal struggle. They recognized the PAST's ability to cast shadows of doubt; some people thought PRESENT's urgency took precedence and some felt the weight of the FUTURE's uncertainties. The battle between these tenses reflected their inner conflicts, each tense vying for dominance.

With the wisdom from the previous discussions lingering in the air, PAST, PRESENT, and FUTURE stood united. "As we stand at the crossroads of our journey," their voices harmonized, "*Which of us is causing you the biggest problems right now, and what do you think you need to do about it?*"

Participants were seeking to identify the tense that holds the most significant influence over their current challenges. Some were burdened with the ghosts of the PAST, struggling to break free from past mistakes. Others were weighed down by the frantic demands of the PRESENT, leaving them overwhelmed and drained. And then there were those whose apprehensions about the FUTURE stifled their growth.

With the collective reflections from the previous questions, PAST, PRESENT, and FUTURE gathered together. "*What inspiration or encouragement have you gained from the chapters of our lives called peace and utopia? It invites you to seek wisdom from moments when our tenses merged in harmony.*"

It was an opportunity to draw from the serene moments of the PAST, the moments of presence and fulfillment from the PRESENT, and the visions of the FUTURE. They recalled instances when the tenses intertwined seamlessly, offering a glimpse of the peace and utopia that could be achieved within themselves.

With the culmination of the workshop's exploration drawing near, PAST, PRESENT, and FUTURE exuded an air of collective understanding. Their voices resonated in unison. "We offer a final question: *How else can we help you?* This extends an open hand, an opportunity for you to seek further guidance and support from PAST, PRESENT, and FUTURE personifications."

In response to this question, participants shared their thoughts and concerns. Some sought guidance on navigating challenging situations rooted in the past, while others sought strategies for living more fully in the present. Some yearned for insights on setting meaningful goals for the future. The room transformed into a sanctuary of introspection as attendees embraced the wisdom and perspectives offered by the tenses.

As the workshop drew close, participants departed with a renewed sense of connection to the tenses that shape their lives. PAST, PRESENT, and FUTURE personifications had served as guides through the intricate web of time, helping them understand the interplay of their lives' chapters. Armed with newfound insights, they walked away leading to a more balanced, mindful, and purposeful journey ahead.

ABOUT THE AUTHOR

Michael is a serial intellectual. He creates intellectual products that transform people and change the world. He was born in Los Angeles and lived there for almost four decades. In 2009, he moved to Baltimore City and has lived there for fourteen years. Michael has five beautiful adult children. Michael has a bachelor's degree in political studies with an emphasis in philosophy as well as a master's degree in divinity.

He is a certified Enneagram administrator, Scrum master and trained in project management. Michael has been coaching and consulting for twenty-five years. He has founded and led multiple nonprofit organizations. Michael is the author of six books; *100 Meditations: An Everyday Book for Everyday People; Don't Plant, Be Planted; Metamorphic Dictis; Be You; Social Revolution is Baltimore's Only Solution;* and *Hard Questions.* Michael is also the creator of the three personal development tools: Pause exercise, Emotional MRI, and Strategic Affirmations.

Michael is an accomplished triathlete and has completed all four distances. Michael's favorite sport is motocross, his favorite fast food is In-N-Out Burger, he is addicted to fresh Reese's Peanut Butter Cups, and absolutely love rottweilers. His favorite animals are killer whales and tigers. One of his favorite authors is Mark Twain, and one of his favorite quotes from him is "The two most important days of your life are the day you are born and the day you find out why."